NOW for ENGLISH 2

COURSE BOOK

KEITH JOHNSON

Nelson

Revision

Number one. Who's this?
It's Sam.

Rainbow Farm

Whose is this book?
It's Fred's.
Is it Fred's book?
Yes, it is.

UNIT 2
Revision

Which animals are the same colour?

What colour is the cow?
It's red.

This cow is red and that cow is green.

Tinker, tailor

Circus Time

Number one. What is he?
He's a juggler.
Number fourteen. What are they?
They're jugglers.

UNIT 3
Revision

At the Zoo

Are they snakes?
Yes they are.
No they aren't.

Snakes live next door and fish live next door. What are they?

Does Kate like
pop music?
Yes, she does.

Do you like pop music?
Yes, I do.

Mrs Porter's kitchen

Look for one minute. Then close your book. Can you remember?

Is there any chocolate in the kitchen?
No, there isn't any.

How many sandwiches are there?
There are four.

We're late

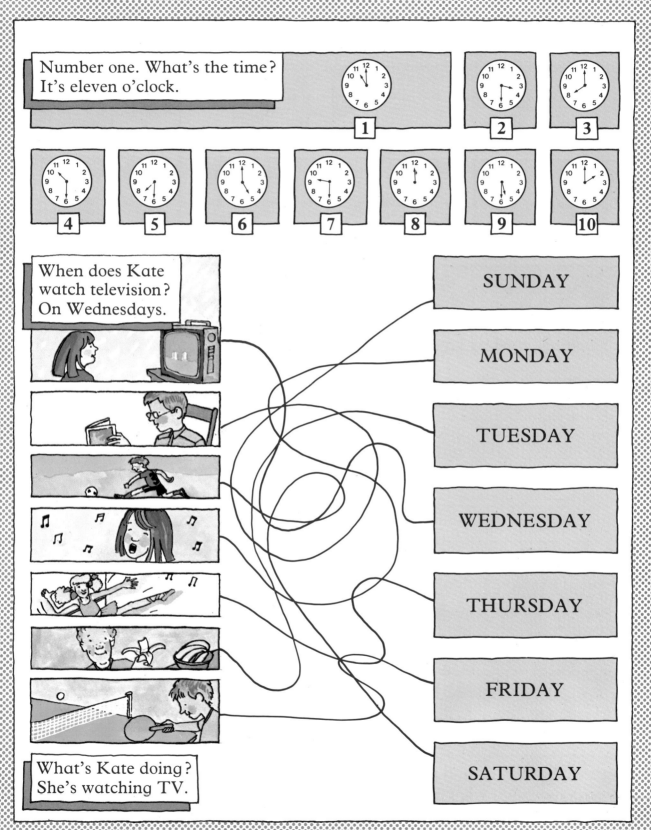

Has Sam got a kite?
Yes, he has.

Who is it? Read and decide.

I've got a kite and a jigsaw. But I haven't got a doll. I've got an apron too. I haven't got a doll's house. I've got a mouth organ and a puppet. I've got some football boots too. Am I Kate or Fred, or Chris or Sally?

Now write about Kate.
I've got a . . .

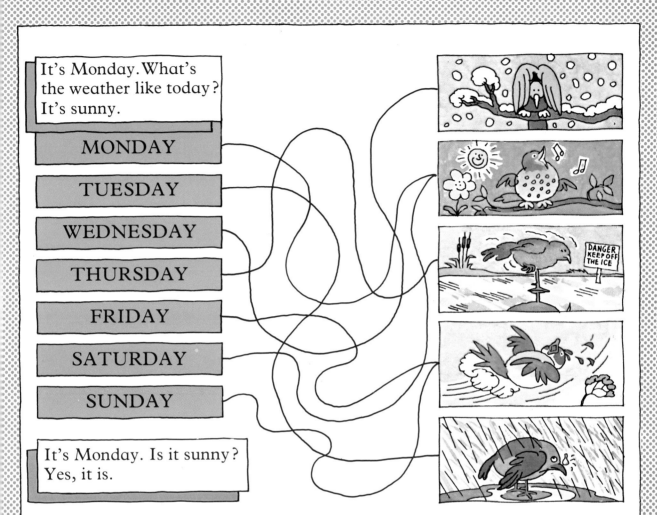

It's Monday. What's the weather like today? It's sunny.

MONDAY

TUESDAY

WEDNESDAY

THURSDAY

FRIDAY

SATURDAY

SUNDAY

It's Monday. Is it sunny? Yes, it is.

It never happens

UNIT 6

Games to play

Find the photos

Jane's
running.

Mr Porter's
flying a kite.

Sam's
sweeping
the floor.

Bella's
sleeping.

Mrs Porter's
making
the bed.

Chris is
flying a kite.

Chris is
playing
football.

Sam's playing
football.

START

Mr Porter's sweeping the floor.

Jane's sleeping.

Jane's playing football.

Chris is making the bed.

Mrs Porter's singing.

Sam's flying a kite.

UNIT 7

Welcome back

Read this and then complete Debbie's timetable in the Activity Book p. 26.

This is Debbie Whitmore. She's nine years old and she lives in England. Her school starts at nine o'clock and she goes home at a quarter to four. She's good at Maths. She's got Maths on Mondays at eleven o'clock, on Tuesdays at nine o'clock, on Wednesdays at half-past one, on Thursdays at nine o'clock and on Fridays at half-past one.
She's good at Music too. She's got Music on Tuesdays at a quarter to three, and on Fridays at eleven o'clock.

When has she got English?

When has she got Art?

When has she got Games?

When has she got History?

When has she got Geography?

When has she got Swimming?

UNIT 8

Little brown Ben

Which puppy is brown?
The little one.

A little
brown puppy.

A big
white puppy.

A little
black kitten.

A big
white kitten.

Good morning. Can I help you?

We want to buy a kitten, please.

Oh look, Mum.
Look at that puppy.

Which one?

The little brown one.

He's barking at me.
He's saying 'Take me home'.

But we're buying a kitten,
Sally. Which ones do you like?
The black ones or the white ones?

I don't want a kitten now, Mum.
I want this puppy. Look, he's
licking me.

Oh all right, Sally.
Let's take the puppy.

Hurray. Come on
little brown Ben.

Our pets

My name's Mary.
I've got a pet parrot.
Her name's Polly and she's green and yellow.
Polly can speak.
What does Polly like?

I'm John.
I've got a pet mouse.
Her name's Minny, and she's white.
Minny can squeak.
What does Minny like?

My name's Peter.
I've got a pet puppy.
His name's Scamp.
Scamp is brown and he can bark.
What does Scamp like?

I'm Anne, and I've got a pet kitten.
Her name's Kitty.
Kitty is black.
She can miaow.
What does Kitty like?

What do Polly, Minny, Scamp and Kitty like?
Answer in the Activity Book p. 30.

fish

cheese

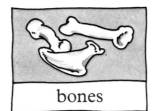
bones

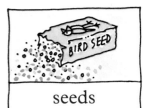
seeds

UNIT 9

Chris' super cake

What's Chris going to do?
He's going to put butter in the basin.

1 BUTTER

2 SUGAR

3 EGGS

4 FLOUR

5 EAT

Sam, I'm going to make a cake. Do you want to help?

Sorry Chris. I'm going to watch TV. And I'm not hungry.

All right. But it's going to be a super cake.

...with jam and lots of cream. And I'm going to eat it all.

Let's see. First put butter and sugar in the bowl. Mix. Add eggs and flour. Mix together.

Oops. Oh no!

Poor Bella.

Bella, come back. Oh dear. Mum's going to be very angry.

Tanya is helping her mother.
They're going to make an omelette.
This is Tanya's recipe:

An omelette

Break three eggs in a bowl.
Add some salt and some cheese.
Mix together.
Put some butter in the frying pan.
Turn on the cooker.
When the butter is very hot, put the eggs,
cheese and salt in the frying pan.
Cook for two minutes.

Can you put the pictures in order?
Write in the Activity Book p. 34.

UNIT 10

Our lucky day

60	61	63	67	69
70	72	74	76	78
80	81	85	88	89
90	92	94	95	97
		100		

Chris and Sam's family are driving in the country ...

There's no petrol. Oh no! What are we going to do?

Look. I can see a man coming. Perhaps he can help.

Excuse me. How far away is the town?

The town? It's about seventy kilometres away.

Seventy kilometres!

It's all right, everyone. I can see a petrol station. It's about one kilometre away.

But we can't push the car one kilometre.

Don't worry. We can drive there without petrol.

Jump in everybody.

We're very lucky.

Yes. It's our lucky day.

This is Mr Clark.
He lives in a town.
It's called Maidenhead.
How far is it from Maidenhead
to London?
It's about fifty kilometres.
Mr Clark lives in a flat.

This is John Andrews.
He lives in a village.
It's called Goring.
How far is it from Goring to
London?
It's about seventy kilometres.
John lives in a farmhouse.

This is Suzanne Roberts.
She lives in a city.
It's called Oxford.
How far is it from Oxford to
London?
It's about ninety kilometres.
Suzanne Roberts lives in a house.

There's a map in the Activity Book on p. 38. Can you complete it?

UNIT 11

Frankenstein's uncle

What's Sam and Chris' phone number?
Six, nine, oh, double one.

Sam and Chris	69011
Kate	52237
Fred	42990
Miss Scott	70196
Mr White	63744

Fred, do you want to go to the cinema this evening?

Oh yes! There's a horror film on.

'Frankenstein's Uncle'! I want to see that.

All right. Let's phone Sam and Chris.

Sam's reading this evening, I bet. He reads all the time.

Six, nine, oh, double one.

Hello. Is that Mrs Porter?

Yes, it is.

It's Sally here.

Hello, Sally. Chris and Sam are at the cinema.

You see, Fred. Sam doesn't read all the time.

This is Stephen.
He's nine.
What does he do in his spare time?
In the evenings he often watches TV.
He likes the cinema and the theatre.
On Saturdays he sometimes goes ice skating, but he never plays football.
His hobby is stamp collecting.
He's got hundreds of stamps.

This is Stephen's sister.
Her name's Jenny and she's eleven.
What does she do in her spare time?
She likes animals.
She's got a cat and a dog.
She often goes to the zoo and to the circus.
On Saturdays she plays basketball, and she goes horse riding too.
She likes music.
She can play the violin.

There's a table in the Activity Book on p. 42. Can you complete it?

Spell it

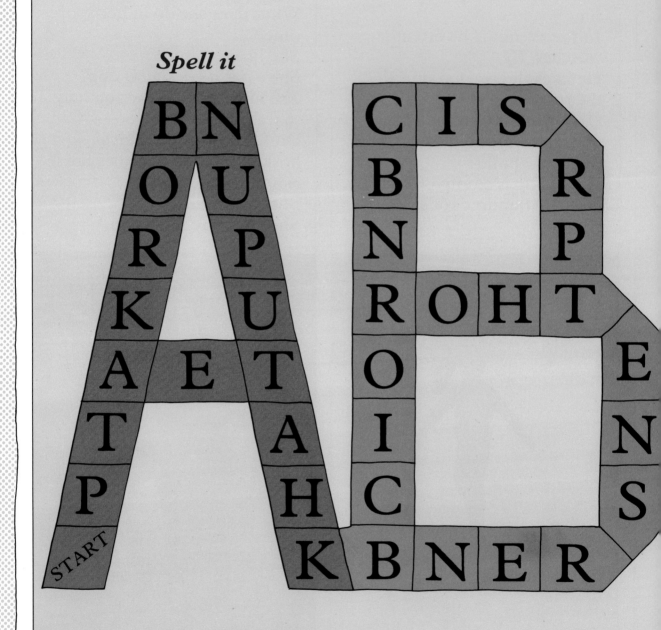

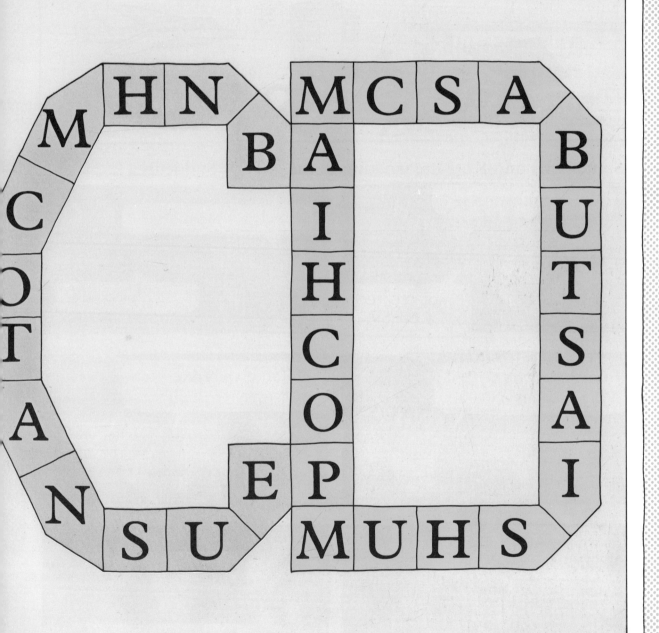

UNIT 13
Chris' monster

Do you remember?
Look at the Course Book p. 10.

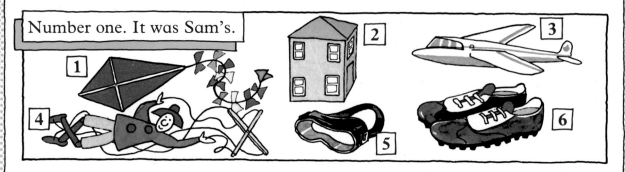

Number one. It was Sam's.

Sam, Chris and Kate are walking in the woods. Suddenly . . .

What was that noise?

It was a scream. Where's Chris?

Chris, what's the matter?

A...a...a monster!

First, there was a hand. A big, cold hand.

Then there were two black legs. It was horrible.

Where was it, Chris? Show us.

Over there.

Oh Chris! It wasn't a monster. Look. It's a tree.

Make Monster Man

First make Monster Man's body.

Make two arms and two legs.

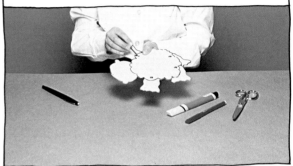

What colour is Monster Man? He's green.

He's got two ears, a nose and a mouth. He's got one eye.

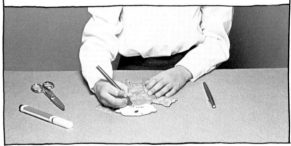

Has he got any hair? Yes. Here it is.

Monster Man is ready.

Now look at the Activity Book p. 48.

UNIT 14

Going away

Did Kate go to the cinema?
Yes, she did.

The Porter family are going away for two days . . .

Come on, Mum. We're late.

I'm ready.

Mum, did you lock the door?

Yes, I did. Of course I did, Chris.

Dad, did you close the windows?

Yes Sam, I did, don't worry.

Wait a minute. Stop the car.

What's the matter?

Mum, did you put Bella in the car?

Dad, did you put Bella in the car?

No, we didn't.

We didn't bring Bella. Quick. Let's go back.

It's nine o'clock.

Mr and Mrs Roberts are going to the country for two weeks.
They're going by car.
The journey takes four hours.

Where are the Andrews family going?
They're going on holiday to France.
The journey takes seven hours.
They're going by train and by boat.

The Robinsons are going to Switzerland.
Their journey takes only two hours.
How are they going?
By plane of course.
They're on holiday.

Jane and Andrew aren't going by plane.
They're going by bicycle.
They're going to the mountains and their journey takes eleven hours.
How far is it to the mountains?
About eighty kilometres.

When are they going to arrive?
Look at the Activity Book p. 52.

UNIT 15

The big green martian

Fred was in his spaceship. It landed on Mars ... What happened?

In space

Who was the first man in space?
It was Yuri Gagarin.
His spaceship was called
Vostok I.
It was launched in April 1961.
He was in space for two hours.

This is Aleksey Leonov.
He walked in space.
His spaceship was called
Voskhod 2.

Neil Armstrong was the first
man on the moon.
He walked on the moon in
1969.
His spaceship was called
Apollo 11.

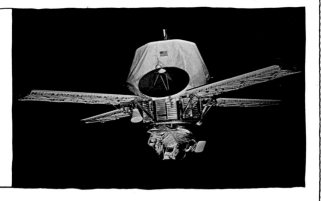

This is Mariner 6.
It was launched in 1969.
Where did Mariner 6 go?
To Mars, but it didn't land
there.
How far is it to Mars?
The journey takes 157 days.

Now look at the Activity Book p. 56.

UNIT 16

Sam's dinner

Number one. Nineteen sixty-nine.

1969	1961	1974
1	2	3

1957	1836	1789	1693	1502
4	5	6	7	8

Sam, there's a programme about Neil Armstrong on TV.

All right. I'm coming.

Hurry up. It started ten minutes ago.

I'm finishing my dinner.

In 1969 Armstrong walked on the moon.

Come on, Sam. You're missing the programme.

Just a minute.

Here I am.

But Sam. It's half past eight. The programme finished fifteen minutes ago.

Oh dear! Then I'm going to have another cake.

How old?

Debbie started school when she was five.
She started school four years ago.
How old is she? She's nine.

When did Anne buy her pet kitten?
When she was nine.
That was one year ago.
How old is she?

Suzanne Roberts started living in Oxford when she was twenty-one.
She started living in Oxford four years ago. How old is she?

Stephen started collecting stamps four years ago.
He started collecting stamps when he was five.
How old is he?

When did Jane and Andrew go to the mountains?
Two years ago, when they were sixteen.
How old are they?

Neil Armstrong was born in 1930.
When did he go to the moon?
In 1969.
How old was he?

Now look at the Activity Book p. 60.

UNIT 17
Wake up, Sally

Number one didn't play tennis, didn't watch television, didn't walk in the woods, didn't mend the car. Who is it?

It's Monday morning . . .

Sally and Kate. What did you do yesterday?

We visited my uncle.

He lives in the country.

What did you do there?

We played tennis.

And we walked in the woods.

What time did you go to bed, Sally?

At eleven o'clock.

And I didn't sleep very well.

Yes, I can see that.

Wake up, Sally.

What did Martin and Pauline
do yesterday?
They were in the country.
Did they go by car?

First they climbed a hill.
It was very steep.
What happened?

They stopped next to a river.
Martin wanted to catch a fish.
What happened?

They walked in a field.
They wanted to have a picnic.
What happened?

Pauline collected some flowers.
Martin carried the flowers
home.
What happened?

Now look at the Activity Book p. 64.

Games to play

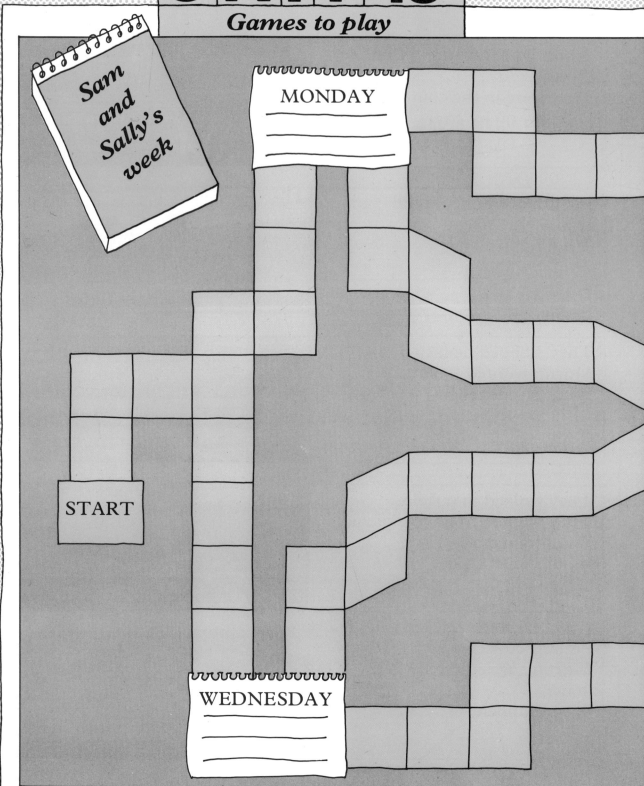

Sam and Sally's week

MONDAY

START

WEDNESDAY

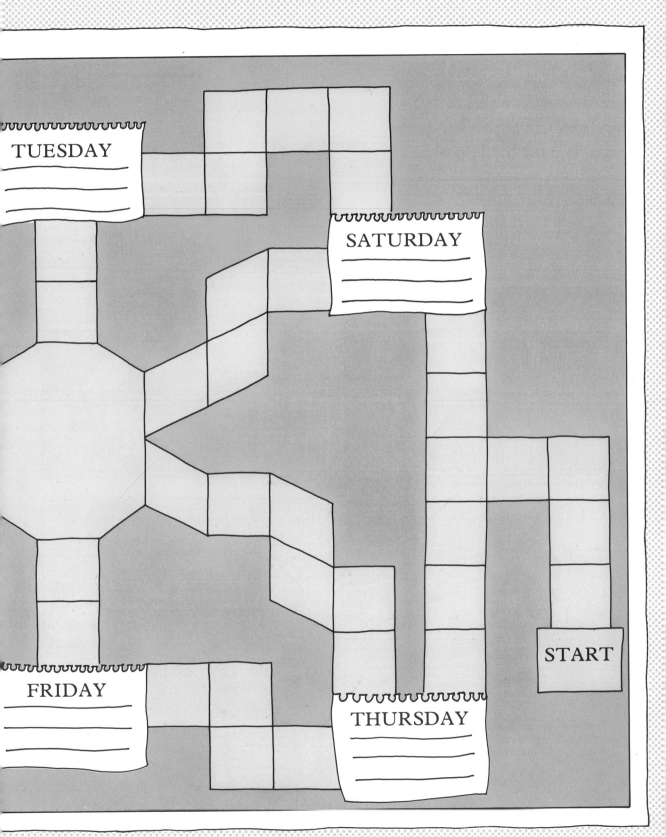

UNIT 19

Sam's new radio

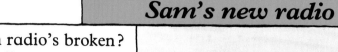

Which radio's broken?
The yellow one.

£15

£95

Look, Dad. My radio's broken. My beautiful, old radio.

Don't worry, Sam. We can buy another one.

Hurray.

Which one do you like, Sam? I like this one.

This one's nice.

It's very expensive. It's too expensive. Here's a cheap one.

But it's too small.

I like the expensive one. And Bella likes it too.

All right. Let's buy it. It's a present for you and Bella.

The high street

This is George.
He works in the electrician's.
He sells TVs, radios and
record players.
The electrician's is next to the
police station.

Sharon works in the baker's.
She sells bread and rolls.
She sells cakes as well.
The baker's is between the
electrician's and the
supermarket.

This is Michael.
Michael works in the
butcher's, next to the shoe
shop.
It sells meat.

Jane works in the sweet shop,
between the supermarket and
the butcher's.
What does her shop sell?
Sweets and chocolates, of
course.

Now look at the Activity Book p. 70.

UNIT 20

Poor, old Chris

Whose radio is older? Kate's.

Sam is showing Kate his new radio . . .

Here's a map of the world.

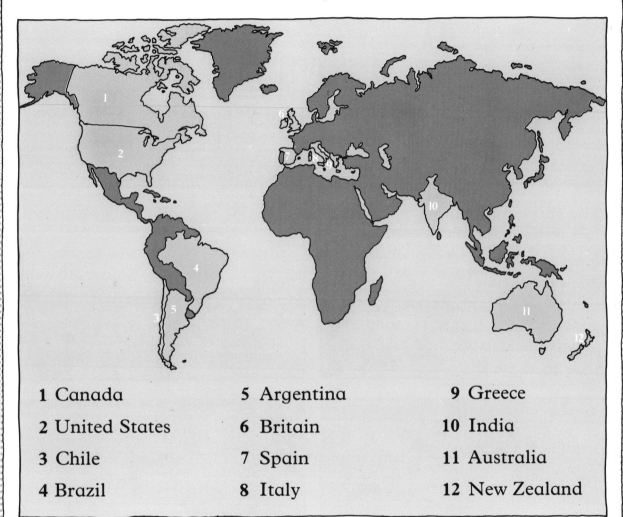

1 Canada	**5** Argentina	**9** Greece
2 United States	**6** Britain	**10** India
3 Chile	**7** Spain	**11** Australia
4 Brazil	**8** Italy	**12** New Zealand

Find Brazil, Argentina and Chile.

Find the United States and Canada.

Find Britain, Italy, Spain and Greece.

Where's India?

Where are Australia and New Zealand?

Now look at the Activity Book p. 74.

UNIT 21
Ready, steady, go

Who was first? Ben.

The children are going to have a race . . .

Ready, steady, go.

I want Bella to win. Come on Bella.

Bella's going to be second or third. Sally's going to win.

Poor, old Ben. Look, he's last.

Be careful everyone. Oh, too late.

You see, Sam. Ben wasn't last. He was first.

Here's your prize, Ben.

It was sports day at Debbie's school yesterday. It was like the Olympic Games. Debbie was Britain. Sylvia was Brazil. Anne was Argentina. John was Spain. Peter was Italy. Fred was Greece.

Debbie Sylvia Anne Spain Italy Greece

Here are some results.

In the high jump, Debbie was first.
Peter was second and Anne was third.

In the hurdles, Sylvia was first and Fred was second.
John was third.

In the gymnastics, Anne was first.
Fred was second and Debbie was third.

Here are the results of the long jump: 1st John
2nd Peter
3rd Sylvia

Now look at the Activity Book, p. 78.

43

UNIT 22
Going to the theatre

Number one. You mustn't turn left. You must go straight on.

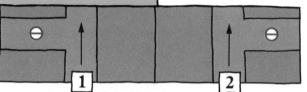

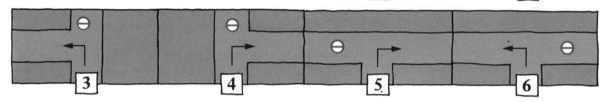

The Porter family are going to the theatre.

Hurry up, Mum. We mustn't be late.

Turn left at the traffic lights, Dad.

But I can't turn left. I must go straight on.

Here we are. The theatre's in this street.

Are you sure, Sam?

Yes, I am. But you mustn't park here, Dad. You can park over there. On the right.

NO PARKING

Sam

Yes, Dad.

Swimming Pool

This isn't the theatre. Look. It's the swimming pool.

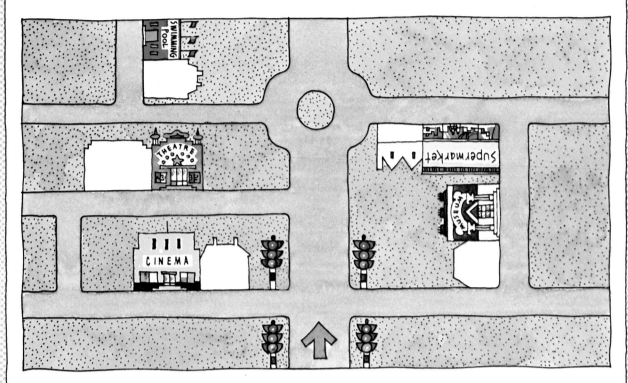

1 Where's the police station? Go to the traffic lights and turn left. It's on the right.

2 Where's the fire station? Go to the roundabout and turn right. It's on the right.

3 Where's the bank? Go to the traffic lights and turn right. Then turn left. It's on the left.

4 Where's the school? Go to the traffic lights and go straight on. Then turn left. It's on the right.

5 Where's the hospital? Go to the roundabout and turn left. Then turn right. It's on the right.

Now look at the Activity Book p. 82.

UNIT 23
The fierce dog

1 Monday. Fourth, eleventh, twenty-fifth.

	JANUARY				
MON	...	4	11	18	25
TUE	...	5	12	19	26
WED	...	6	13	20	27
THU	...	7	14	21	28
FRI	1	8	15	22	29
SAT	2	9	16	23	30
SUN	3	10	17	24	31

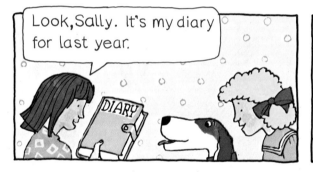

Martin and Pauline are visiting their uncle.
Pauline writes a letter to their mother.

26th July.

Dear Mum,

It's wonderful here. Yesterday we went to the fair. First we
went on the roundabout. My horse was yellow. Then Martin
won a balloon — a red one. Afterwards we went down the
slide. I was very frightened, and Martin was frightened too.
Martin went on the big wheel next, but I didn't want to go
on it. We both went on the bumper cars. I chased Martin in
my car. Then we went on the ghost train. We saw lots of
ghosts and monsters.
We don't want to come home. Can we stay here until Friday?

Love, Pauline.

Can you put the pictures in order?
Write in the Activity Book p. 86.

On the ghost train

GHOST TRAIN

IN

UNIT 25

The tree house

Who will phone Kate, Fred and Sally?
Chris will phone Kate, Fred and Sally.

What shall we do today, Sam?

I know. Let's make a tree house.

Good idea. I'll phone the others.

And I'll get some nails and a hammer.

What will you do, Kate?

Shall I saw the wood?

All right.

Be careful. It'll fall down.

No, it won't. Don't worry.

There. It's finished.

What a lovely tree house, children! But Chris...

Yes, Mum?

It hasn't got a roof. You'll get very wet.

Hello. I'm Tom Kelly.
This is my house.
It's got six rooms.
A living room, a kitchen, three bedrooms and a bathroom.
It's got a garage too.

Here's the hall and the stairs.
The bedroom and the bathroom are upstairs.
The other rooms are downstairs.

This is my bedroom.
It's smaller than the other bedrooms, but it's bigger than the bathroom.
The curtains are brown.
That's my guitar on the bed.

This is the kitchen.
It's smaller than the living room, of course.
The door goes into the garden.
We've got a small garden.

Now look at the Activity Book p. 92.

Chris and the spider

 My name's Peter. My favourite animal is the horse.
I go horse riding every week.
I'm scared of spiders and I don't like rats.

  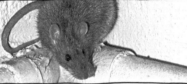

 Hello. I'm Mary. I'm scared of spiders too.
I don't like bats either. They're very ugly.
My favourite animal is the giraffe. I like his long neck.

  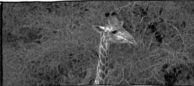

 My name's John. I like giraffes too.
And zebras. But I don't like snakes or toads.
They're horrible.

 I'm Anne. I like elephants.
When I go to the zoo, I always ride on an elephant.
I'm scared of rhinos. They're very dangerous.

Now look at the Activity Book p. 96.

UNIT 27

Ben's bed

Number one. It looks like a bicycle. But it isn't a bicycle.

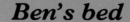

Number one. It isn't a bicycle. But it looks like a bicycle.

What a funny noise! It's coming from your bag, Sally.

It sounds like a baby crying.

It feels like a scarf. Or a furry glove.

I didn't bring my scarf or gloves today. Let's open the bag and see.

It looks like a puppy.

It is a puppy. It's Ben.

My bag looks like his bed at home.

And he was sleeping in your bag. Poor, old Ben.

Shapes

Here are two circles. One is pink and the other is green.

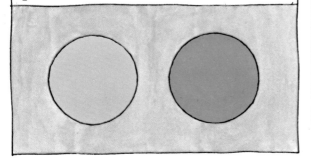

How many round shapes can you see in the picture?

Here are two squares. One is orange and the other is brown.

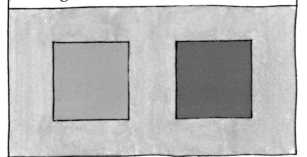

How many square shapes can you see in the picture?

Here are two triangles. One is purple and the other is yellow.

How many triangular shapes can you see in the picture?

Now look at Activity Book p. 100.

I'm Kate. Give me a sweet please, Sam.

I've got a secret.

A secret?

Come on, Fred. Tell me.

Yes, tell us.

Give me a sweet and I'll tell you.

But I've only got one left.

Give him the sweet, Sam.

All right. But you promise you'll tell us.

Yes.

There's a school trip next week. Miss Scott told me.

We're going to the seaside.

Hurray!

We'll have a lovely time!

It's Jane and Alan's school trip tomorrow.
Jane's looking for her swimsuit.
Here it is.

Alan is looking for his bucket and spade.
He likes making big sandcastles in the sand.

Maybe it'll be sunny.
They're taking their sunglasses and an airbed.
They both like sunbathing on the beach.

Maybe it'll rain, Jane thinks.
She's taking an umbrella and a raincoat.
Alan doesn't think it'll rain.
He isn't taking a raincoat or an umbrella.

Now look at the Activity Book p. 104

UNIT 29

Sally's swim

Where's Miss Scott's towel? It's behind the ball.

When Alan and Jane were at the seaside they had a motor boat trip.
It was very exciting.
They saw a man water skiing and another man wind surfing.

They also saw a fishing boat with three fishermen in it.
The boat had a big fishing net.

Alan looked through his binoculars at the beach.
He saw children playing ball and making sandcastles.

When they were near the pier, they waved to a boy and a girl in a rowing boat.
Their mother and father were with them.

Now look at the Activity Book p. 108.

Word List

Unit 7
message
Maths
Music
Art
History
Games
Geography
timetable
back
quite
how do you spell?
welcome
thank you very much
go home
good at

Unit 8
kitten
puppy
boots
pet
parrot
cheese
seeds
brown
black
white
buy
bark at
say
take
lick
speak
squeak
miaow
Can I help you?

Unit 9
jam
cream
bowl
salt
egg
omelette

recipe
butter
frying pan
cooker
first
together
all
angry
help (verb)
add
mix
break
turn on
make a cake
lots of
let's see

Unit 10
petrol
man
town
kilometre
petrol station
flat
village
farmhouse
map
perhaps
about
without
lucky
push
excuse me
it's all right
don't worry
jump in
It's our lucky day.
called
from ... to

Unit 11
(at the) cinema
evening
horror film
uncle

phone
spare time
theatre
ice skating
hobby
stamp collecting
animal
zoo
basketball
horse riding
violin
gangster
cartoon
musical
all the time
you see

Unit 13
scream
leg
woods
body
arm
ear
nose
hair
mouth
eye
horrible
us
show
What's the matter?
over there

Unit 14
window
country (opposite of town)
journey
hour
France
Switzerland
plane
quick
by (car, boat etc.)

how (= by what means
of transport)
arrive
lock
bring
go back
rub out
stop the car

Unit 15
Mars
Martian
moon
million
(in) space
for (a time)
outside
now
attack
happen
land (verb)
launch (some dates)

Unit 16
programme
minute
finish (verb)
miss
born
just a minute (hurry up)
here I am
how long ago?
how old
across/down (in crosswords)

Unit 17
hill
flower
steep
yesterday
well
visit
climb
wake up

go to bed
catch a fish

Unit 19
radio
electrician's
TV
record player
baker's
roll (of bread)
butcher's
shoe shop
sweet shop
broken
beautiful
old
nice
expensive
cheap
small
large
why
work
of course

Unit 20
new
loud
poor (old)
countries

Unit 21
prize
sports day
Olympic Games
result
high jump
hurdles
gymnastics
long jump
last
like = similar to
win
ready, steady, go
be careful

Unit 22
fire station
traffic lights
swimming pool
roundabout (road)
museum
bank
hospital
sure
park
run
then
straight on
on the left/right

Unit 23
diary
fair
ghost train
balloon
slide
month
date
big wheel
bumper car
both
fierce
frightened
afterwards
until
remember
chase

Unit 25
tree house
nail
hammer
wood
children
roof
room
garage
hall
stairs
upstairs

downstairs
curtain
guitar
finished
lovely
go into
get (=fetch)
saw (=cut)
fall down
get wet
there (as exclamation)
the others

Unit 26
neck
toad
rat
bat
giraffe
rhino
zebra
tomorrow
tonight
either
favourite
dangerous
ugly
long
tell
every week

Unit 27
baby
scarf
glove
circle
shape
triangle
furry
the other
round
square
orange (adj)
purple

come from
cry

Unit 28
swimsuit
secret
(school) trip
time (a lovely time)
bucket
spade
sandcastle
sand
sunglasses
airbed
beach
umbrella
raincoat
our
left (remaining)
look for
promise
next week
please
thank you

Unit 29
towel
clothes
motor boat
water skiing
wind surfing
fishing boat

fisherman
fishing net
binoculars
pier
rowing boat
exciting
dry
quickly
near
have a swim
get dry

wave
that's better